Let's Talk About
TEASING

Let's Talk About

TEASING

By JOY BERRY

Illustrated by John Costanza
Edited by Orly Kelly
Designed by Jill Losson

GROLIER ENTERPRISES CORP.

Let's talk about TEASING.

When people annoy you or make fun of you in playful ways, they are TEASING you.

Has anyone ever teased you about the way you *look?*

Has anyone ever teased you about the way you *think* and *feel*?

Has anyone ever teased you about what you *say* or *do?*

Has anyone ever teased you about what you *like* and *don't like?*

Whenever someone teases you, you probably feel frustrated, embarrassed, and "put down."

When someone teases you, you may get upset and become angry.

People who tease often enjoy frustrating and embarrassing others.

They enjoy upsetting others.

Thus, you please the person who is teasing you when you become frustrated or upset.

If you want someone to stop teasing you,
you must not become frustrated. You must not
get embarrassed or become upset.

To make sure that you do not do these things,
you must *ignore* the people who are teasing you.
Do not pay attention to what they are saying.

If it is hard for you to ignore them, *walk away*
from them. Do not stay around them while they
are teasing you.

It is important to treat other people the way you want to be treated.

If you do not like it when other people tease you, you should not tease other people.

It is best not to talk about things that a person does not want anyone to talk about.
You should also not tell another person's secrets.

It is best not to say embarrassing things about another person in front of others.

It is best not to say anything to people that may hurt them.

A good rule to remember is —

If you can't say something nice,
don't say anything at all.

If you do this, you may be sure that
you will not hurt other people.

Teasing may hurt someone, so it is best not to do it.